UNTIL THE
VICTORY IS WON

The Story of One Group of Heroes from D-Day to the End

UNTIL THE VICTORY IS WON

David Allender

War Chronicle
New York

Published in the United States in 2001 by Book-of-the-Month Club, 1271 Avenue of the Americas, New York, NY 10020.

CREDITS

Photos and art (t=top, b=bottom, l=left, r=right)

Stan Dzierga: pgs. 3, 14*r*; Phyllis Streczyk Scheuermann: pgs. 7*b*, 12, and 58; Chuck Solomon: pgs. 7*r*, 17, 18, 27, 31, 33*tr*, 42*t*, 47, 55, 57, 60, 61, 63, 65, 67, 79 and back cover; Eisenhower Library: pg. 8; Tina Spalding Gerteisen: endsheets and pgs. 11*t*, 54, and 55*tl*; Vinny DiGaetano: pgs. 13*b* and 48; Fred Reese: pg. 29*t*; Clarence Colson: pgs. 15*b* and 33*tl*; Scott MacNeill: pgs. 19, 39, 68, 72-73, and 76; Bill Mauldin cartoon reprinted by permission of Bill Mauldin and the Watkins/Loomis Agency: pg. 21; Magnum Photos (Robert Capa): pgs. 24 and 36-37; Mae Colwell: pg. 28; National Guard Armory (Bristol, CT): pg. 35; Corbis: pg. 69*b*; Veterans' Services (Harrison, NJ): pg. 49; Walter Bieder: pgs. 53 and 66; Lil Junas: pg. 59. All other images are from the National Archives.

Photos (listed above) © 2001 by Chuck Solomon

Battle map sources:

History of Naval Operations in World War II, Vol. XI: The Invasion of France and Germany 1944-1945: pg. 16-17; *American Forces in Action series: Omaha Beachhead, 6 June-13 June 1944*: pg. 39; *United States Army in World War II: The European Theater of Operations: Breakout and Pursuit and The Ardennes: Battle of the Bulge*: pg 76.

To all the men who came home,
And those who never returned.

☆ ☆ ☆ ☆ ☆ ☆

A memorial in Normandy is inscribed:
Think not only of their passing;
Remember the glory of their spirit.

Long ago

Long ago there raged the deadliest conflict in the history of the human race. It was the Second World War. An evil man and his nation, Adolf Hitler's Nazi Germany, started the war as they meant to rule the entire world: with terror, enslavement, and genocide.

Mankind's hope was an Allied victory. In early June of 1944, armies of the United States, Britain, and Canada gathered for that purpose. Their mission was to invade the coast of France on D-Day, fight their way to Nazi Germany, and destroy its evil heart.

Among the Allied forces was a small group of ordinary soldiers. They were men of E Company, the 16th Regiment, United States 1st Division.

These men became heroes on 6 June 1944. This is their story.

▲ Flags fly above an old battlefield on the coast of France.

◀ Sgt. Phil Streczyk (standing at the far right, shaking hands with an innkeeper) and other E Company soldiers before D-Day.

An infantry division (the walking boys of the army) had around 15,000 men, 9,000 of whom were combat soldiers. These men were divided into three regiments of 3,000 soldiers each. A regiment had three battalions (of 1,000 men), and each battalion had three rifle companies of around 200 men (plus heavy weapon gunners and other specialists). The smallest unit in a rifle company was the 12-man squad, and three squads made up a platoon or section. In this photo, General George Patton is giving a speech to the 1st Division after the liberation of Sicily.

1ST SECTION, E COMPANY, 2ND BATTALION, 16TH REGIMENT, 1ST DIVISION, V CORPS, FIRST ARMY, 21ST ARMY GROUP

Section Leader: Lt. John Spalding, Kentucky

Assistant Section Leader: Tech. Sgt. Phil Streczyk, New Jersey

Staff Sgt. Curtis Colwell, Kentucky

Staff Sgt. Grant Phelps, New York

Sgt. Fred G. Bisco, New Jersey

Sgt. Hubert W. Blades, Delaware

Sgt. Clarence Colson, New York

Sgt. Kenneth Peterson, New Jersey

Sgt. Joseph W. Slaydon, North Carolina

Sgt. Louis J. Ramundo, Pennsylvania

Pfc. Walter R. Bieder, Ohio

Pfc. Bruce S. Buck, Nebraska

Pfc. Raymond R. Curley, New Jersey

Pfc. Stanley A. Dzierga, Massachusetts

Pfc. Richard J. Gallagher, New York

Pfc. Warren S. Guthrie, Ohio

Pfc. Edwin F. Piasecki, Illinois

Pfc. Richard M. Rath, Pennsylvania

Pfc. Alexander Sakowski, Connecticut

Pfc. Virgil Tilley, Tennesse

Pvt. William B. Brown, Illinois

Pvt. Vincent T. DiGaetano, New York

Pvt. Donald E. Johnson, Ohio

Pvt. Robert E. Lee, New Jersey

Pvt. Raymond L. Long, Maryland

Pvt. Carmen M. Meduri, Pennsylvania

Pvt. Elmer F. Reese, Pennsylvania

Pvt. James O. Renfroe, Tennesse

Pvt. William C. Roper, Alabama

Pvt. Charles Scheurman, New Jersey

Pvt. George H. Bowen, Kentucky

Pvt. Richard Sims, Alabama

Abbreviations of rank: Lt. (lieutenant), Sgt. (sergeant), Pfc. (private first class), Pvt. (private).
Streczyk is *Strees-zik.* Bieder / *Bee-der.* Dzierga / *Jur-ga.* DiGaetano / *Dee-Guh-tano.* Piasecki / *Puh-secki.*

THE MEN

Lt. John Spalding

Before our country was at war, while Europe was in flames, the United States hastily began building an Army. In October of 1940, all males from the ages of 21 through 35 were required to register for possible military service. At local draft boards, men who passed the exams were given a number. Thousands across American had the same number, and they were drafted when it was picked out of a glass tank in Washington, D.C.

Sixteen million men registered. A million of them were drafted. John Spalding wasn't one of them, but he joined the Army anyway. He kissed his wife and young son goodbye, and left his home in Owensboro, Kentucky.

Ten months later, the Japanese attacked Pearl Harbor, Hawaii. Soon Japan, Germany, and Italy all declared war on the United States. The Second World War, as a global conflict, had begun.

Germany was America's strongest enemy, and we were their weakest opponent. America needed years to amass and train enough soldiers for a direct attack on the Nazi heartland. John Spalding spent those years far from the frontline as part of the great build-up. Meanwhile, combat soldiers of the 1st Division helped stop Nazi aggression by invading two continents.

The first D-Day was the invasion of North Africa on 7 November 1942. Then came the invasion of Sicily on 10 July 1943. In the fall of 1943, the 1st Division was secretly shipped from Sicily to England to join the gathering forces. Despite the secrecy, the soldiers knew in their bones that the big one was next. Fresh troops joined the division as reinforcements and replacements for soldiers killed in action. One of the new men was Lt. John Spalding. For him, the war was about to begin.

▲ John Spalding's high school photo. His next classroom was in Officer's Candidate School. Instructors there asked themselves: "Would I be willing to follow this man in battle?" John passed.

▲ A blindfolded Secretary of War, Henry Stimson, draws a number in the Selective Service draft.

◄ Soldiers in training.

▲ Phil Streczyk. The army had no classrooms for sergeants. The best soldiers were promoted based on their ability to take action and lead. Vinny DiGaetano still remembers Streczyk's kindness and strength: "He would yell at us sometimes, but he didn't treat us like a piece of crap. He respected us, and treated us like men. And he didn't want any fighting amongst ourselves: we were are all in it together."

Sgt. Phil Streczyk

Phil Streczyk was a warrior: the most daring fighter his men and officers ever knew.

He was born near East Brunswick, New Jersey, and was one of ten children. Like many kids during the Great Depression, Phil worked full time from an early age. He dropped out of school after the 8th grade to earn money and help his family.

By the time Streczyk was 21, he was a truck driver. Then his draft number was picked and, after months of training, he was shipped overseas.

In Tunisia, North Africa, Streczyk won his first of many medals. His men were trapped and Streczyk risked his life by crossing into the open and attacking the enemy with grenades. He took out two enemy guns and, for his courage, Streczyk was awarded the Silver Star. He mailed it home to his mom.

Streczyk sometimes scared his own men as much as he scared the enemy. "One time in Africa," Clarence Colson remembers, "Streczyk got hold of a German motorcycle, and he came riding that thing like a wild man. Maybe he figured the Good Lord was watching over him, but he just didn't seem to care. We had an awful time keeping a helmet on him. When someone would start shooting at us, everyone would keep their heads down, taking little peeks out of the foxholes. Streczyk would be popping up like a robin."

When the 1st Division reorganized in England, soldiers were shuffled into 32-man sections so that a team could fit in one small landing craft.

Lt. Spalding was the commanding officer of the 1st Section. Sgt. Streczyk was second-in-command. The new men listened carefully to everything the sergeant said. He was brave and, more importantly, he had stayed alive.

Pvt. Vincent "Diggy" DiGaetano

In 1941, the Dodgers were still in Brooklyn and so was Vinny DiGaetano. The Dodgers won the pennant and then lost the World Series to the hated Yankees from the Bronx. Two months later, on Vinny's 18th birthday, the Japanese bombed Peal Harbor.

Vinny wanted to rush off and volunteer for the Army as a paratrooper, but his father said no. The draft age had been lowered to 18 and the Army, his father said, would get him soon enough.

It took a year. In the meantime, Vinny got a factory job making gyroscopes for bombers. Then, on his next birthday, an Army induction notice arrived. It was too late to be a paratrooper. The Army needed riflemen for the infantry, and that's what draftee DiGaetano would be.

Basic training was in Texas, a long way from New York. DiGaetano had never seen a gun before in his life. He never had orders screamed in his face by lunatics with stripes on their shoulders.

After many miserable months in the heat and dust, amidst more kinds of snakes than Vinny knew existed, Pvt. DiGaetano was shipped to England. There he was given the Red One shoulder patch, told to sew it on, and was assigned to Spalding's section.

Fitting in with a veteran unit wasn't easy. "I was very lonely," Vinny says, "I didn't know anybody. The other guys had been through North Africa and Sicily and I was just from Brooklyn."

As one of the biggest of the new guys, Vinny got stuck with a job nobody else wanted. Heavy flamethrowers were used to flush the enemy out of pillboxes (concrete gun emplacements). It weighed more than 70 pounds and shot a long, bright flame. Waving it around was like saying, "Hello, Mr. German. Shoot me please." Vinny would carry a flamethrower on D-Day.

▲ " . . . we here highly resolve that these dead shall not have died in vain . . . " So Abraham Lincoln said of the Union dead at Gettysburg. Here the words apply to Pearl Harbor.

▲ Vinny DiGaetano and his sister, Jean, a year or two before the war.

▶ **Top:** "Soldiers without combat experience must be trained mentally for the shock of battle," the army directed its instructors. This was partly accomplished by the use of live ammunition on training courses.

Center: A flamethrower in action. **Bottom:** A bangalore torpedo, a pipe filled with explosives, is placed under a barbed wire. When detonated, the explosion would tear the wire to pieces. The torpedo was invented by a British soldier in Bangalore, India.

▲ In November 1942, Stan Dzierga's hometown paper ran a picture of draftees. One of Stan's sisters drew an arrow to her brother and wrote, "Find the best looking guy. Our opinion. Bob said handsome *zbøj* [Polish for bandit]." Like many of his generation, Stan grew up in a strong ethnic community and was fortunate to be part of a bilingual family.

Other soldiers

Pvt. Bowen was a medic. He could stop most wounded men from bleeding to death. Infection was a major danger. Dirt, even bits of cloth threads, in a wound could cause as much damage as the bullet itself. Pfc. Buck was the runner to carry messages. Dzierga and Bieder were grenadiers: they had grenade launchers that could snap onto their rifles. Sgt. Colwell and his men would carry bangalore torpedoes to blow gaps in the wire barriers.

Sgt. Colson was in charge of the mortars. Colson's main gunner, Pvt. Sims, and another soldier would carry the mortar guns and ammo. Pfc. Tilley and another man would carry BARs (Browning Automatic Rifles, a type of light machine gun). Sergeants Peterson and Blades were bazooka men. Pvt. Reese was Peterson's assistant and, like all the other men in the section, he'd carry ammunition, his rifle, and other supplies.

There were many training exercises on the Dorset coast of England. Then, one day in May 1944, the training was over.

The wait

On 11 May, soldiers were sealed off from the outside world. There'd be no more evenings in pubs or suppers with local families. One officer, Lt. Duckworth, just had time to marry an English girl before the camp gates were locked.

No one knew the date of D-Day. Waiting was terrible. Everyone was on edge. Lt. Spalding couldn't sleep at night. He was supposed to lead men in combat. He was responsible for their lives. He hid his fear and tried acting tough until his superior, Captain Wozenski, chewed him out in front of everybody. Spalding could only pray he would prove himself when it counted most.

Mail was allowed in, but not allowed out. Sometimes letters made the men feel worse. Fred Bisco got one from his girlfriend back home. She couldn't wait for the war to be over and had

▲ Clarence Colson was with E Company before Pearl Harbor. He had left his family's dairy farm in January 1941 and volunteered for the Army. Clarence became part of the heavy weapon platoon and, as a sergeant, led a mortar squad. A mortar gun is like a small cannon, fired from a tripod. Clarence is standing in the second row at the right before the war in Fort Devens, Massachusetts.

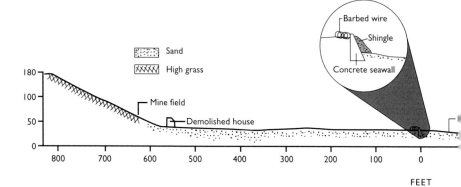

Soldiers on the march in Dorset, England.

Which of the following best describes your own feeling about getting into combat against the Germans?

A) I'd like to get into the fight as soon as I can

B) I'm ready to go when my turn comes

C) I'd just as soon stay out of combat if possible

D) I don't want to get into combat at all

Soldiers were surveyed by the army's Research Branch in April and May 1944. Among replacement soldiers, 56% chose **A** or **B** (mostly **B**). Among veterans, only 32% chose **A** or **B** (and very few chose **A**). The survey was to gauge morale: everyone went, including men who chose **D**.

found someone else, so the letter said goodbye. Fred was heartbroken and his friends were outraged. What were they fighting for if this was the thanks they got? Vinny DiGaetano received a letter from his sister. Their father was dead: he had been on his way to work and suffered a fatal heart attack. DiGaetano asked for permission to call home, and the request was denied.

From 25 May, no one would get any more letters; all incoming mail was impounded until further notice. Then the soldiers were told the biggest secret of World War II. They would be making a full-frontal assault on a beach in Normandy, France. Their beach was code-named Omaha.

The plan was simple. In the middle of the night, the invaders would leave the transport and be carried 11 miles in landing craft. As close to shore as possible, the ramps would go down. Soldiers with heavy loads would wade through freezing water that was studded with mined obstacles. On the beach, they would face hundreds of yards of open ground broken only by barbed wire and dotted with landmines. Enemy machine guns, artillery, and mortar would keep the Americans in crossfire with every step.

There was no other way to invade, but the 1st Division veterans wondered why they had to be the ones to do it. The United States Army had eight million people in uniform, and 75% of them would never be in combat. Why couldn't all those other guys do their share? Instead, on 31 May, the gates of the camp swung open. To the sergeant's cadence of "Hup, two, three, four" the 1st

Division soldiers marched to Portland harbor. The dock swarmed with men and vehicles as E and F Company boarded the troop ship *Henrico*. Then, on 5 June, at about 6:00 p.m., the ship weighed anchor and joined the huge convoy bound for France.

Capt. Ed Wozenski gave his men a final briefing. Their mission was to destroy a German strongpoint on top of a hill overlooking Omaha. Then they'd push through the Germans in a village called Colleville.

D-Day was tomorrow, 6 June. H-Hour was 6:30 a.m. Reveille aboard ship would be at 3:00 a.m.

"Now the fine people of the air force have promised," Wozenski said, "to blast the strongpoint with 186 tons of bombs. Don't depend on it. Remember Sicily?" Heads nodded. For the new guys, the captain told how trigger-happy American gunners shot down our own planes, loaded with paratroopers. E Company ended up facing a German tank attack alone. He didn't mention his own heroics; how he let a German tank rumble over his foxhole then jumped up and blasted it from behind with a bazooka while calmly shouting orders. "Only have faith," Wozenski went on, "in what you have in your own hands, your weapons and communications. One more thing: First son-of-a-gun on top of that hill set off a yellow-smoke flare. Everyone else, look for that signal."

It would be a short night, and the captain advised everyone to get some sleep.

▲ Soldiers exited a landing craft via the ramp in front. The ramp was lowered, and raised again for the return trip by the coxswain, a navy pilot.

◀ The drawing shows the basic terrain of Omaha beach. Invading soldiers must cross hundreds of yards while in the sights of enemy guns. The invaders had three major things on their side: the guns of navy warships, airforce bombers, and (a super secret weapon) amphibious tanks. If all went as planned, the Germans would be blasted off the hill and the invaders could walk right into Normandy.

TYPICAL TERRAIN SECTION
OMAHA BEACH

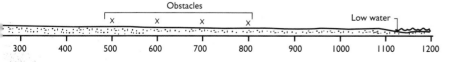

Obstacles

Low water

300 400 500 600 700 800 900 1000 1100 1200

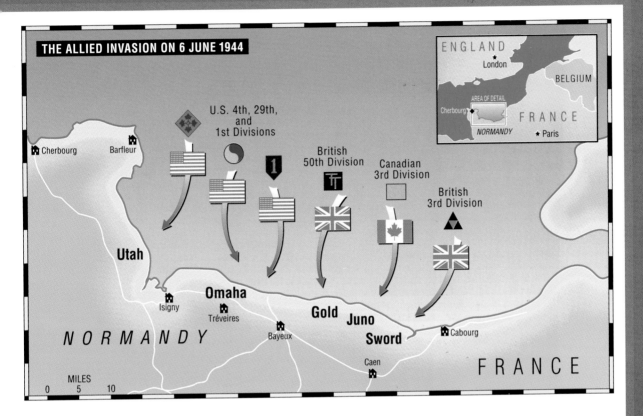

THE ALLIED INVASION ON 6 JUNE 1944

U.S. 4th, 29th, and 1st Divisions

British 50th Division

Canadian 3rd Division

British 3rd Division

Cherbourg
Barfleur

Utah

Isigny

Omaha

Tréveires

Gold Juno

Bayeux

Sword

Cabourg

N O R M A N D Y

Caen

FRANCE

MILES
0   5   10

ENGLAND
London

BELGIUM

AREA OF DETAIL

Cherbourg

FRANCE

NORMANDY   Paris

Normandy

is a province on the Channel coast of France. High ground overlooks the stretch of beach code-named Omaha. On D-Day, German gunners and fields of landmines made Omaha a perfect deathtrap.

The fifty-mile front was divided into five invasion beaches. American soldiers would assault Utah and Omaha; Gold and Sword were assigned to the British; and Juno beach to Canadian soldiers. In addition to infantry, paratroopers would land behind Utah and Sword beaches.

Omaha beach itself was four miles long and broken into sectors of Charlie, Dog, Easy, and Fox (subdivided into areas with color codenames). The 16th Regiment of the 1st Division was responsible for two sectors of the beach. E and F Company were planned to be the first assault wave on sector Easy Red.

H-HOUR COUNTDOWN

H minus three and 40 minutes / 2:50 a.m.

Eleven miles off the invasion shore, transport ships dropped anchor. Soldiers were roused for assembly. Soon sergeants shouted the order, "pick it up and put it on." Everyone started loading up.

At the last minute, Pvt. Fred Reese had an idea. He grabbed a big roll of toilet paper and stuck it under his helmet.

H minus three to two / 3:30 to 4:30 a.m.

The sea was very rough. Waves were three to four feet high, some even reached six feet. Pfc. Wally Bieder was one of the first men down the side and into the landing craft. He held the bottom of the rope ladder for the other solders as the craft bucked up and down. Lt. Spalding took his place at the front of the craft, behind the ramp. Next to him was Sgt. Fred Bisco.

When all the men were aboard, equipment was lowered from the ship's deck by rope. Pvt. Vinny DiGaetano saw the flame-thrower come twisting down. The craft banged and scraped against the side of the ship and a careless hand or foot could be smashed to a pulp. He grabbed the weapon and strapped it to his back.

Fully loaded, the craft circled until finally the order came: "All boats away!"

H minus one and 15 minutes / 5:15 a.m.

It was sunrise. If you were a commander looking down from a helicopter, you would expect to see five neat columns of landing craft moving like slow arrows that would reach shore precisely at 6:30 a.m.

But if you had looked down at first light, you would see boats

▲ "When ya hit th' water swish yer feet around. They kin use it." This is a cartoon by 45th Division soldier Bill Mauldin.

▲ Landing craft awaiting the order to depart.

◀ Warships of the U.S. Navy.

Colonel George Taylor, commanding officer of the 16th Regiment, briefed war correspondents (bound to secrecy) aboard the ships. "The first six hours will be the toughest," he said. "That is when we will be weakest. But we've got to open the door. Somebody has to lead the way. And if we fail, then the troops behind us will do the job. They'll just keep throwing stuff onto the beaches until something breaks. That is the plan."

▼ Soldiers head for shore. The coxswain steers from a raised platform at the back of the craft. Behind him are machine gunners.

in clusters and veering off course. In the words of historian Samuel Eliot Morison: "You would have assumed that something was going wrong, and you would have been right."

H minus one / 5:30 a.m.

Amphibious tanks were supposed to protect the infantry. Thirty were launched in a rougher sea than the tanks were designed to handle. One after the other floundered in the high waves and sank to the bottom of the English Channel.

H minus 40 minutes / 5:50 a.m.

The coast erupted as a fleet of navy warships opened fire. Two ships pounded Easy Red and the strongpoints above the beach.

H minus 30 minutes / 6:00 a.m.

Four hundred and eighty bombers were scheduled to hit the coastal defenses with 1,285 tons of bombs. Due to heavy cloud cover, aircrews could not see the targets. There was a risk of hitting landing craft so bombardiers were ordered to delay bomb drops by thirty seconds. The bombs fell on schedule but they landed far from the beach. Some hit French farms three miles inland.

Meanwhile, within thick walls of concrete and iron, German gunners checked their weapons and waited.

H minus 15 minutes / 6:15 a.m.

In the growing light, Spalding got his first glimpse of shore. He peered around the ramp and was hit with a wave of cold salt water. His feet slipped but he caught himself before he crashed into Sgt. Bisco.

All the men were drenched from the sea spray and the cold morning mist. Seawater pushed islands of vomit around the landing craft floor. Some men had begun throwing up from the time they entered the craft. The Army had issued "Bag, Vomit" but these were full. Soldiers jammed in together spewed on each other.

H minus three minutes / 6:27 a.m.

When landing craft were five hundred yards from shore, the final phase of the bombardment began. Hundreds of rockets were launched at Easy Red. They arched impressively through the air and fell short, exploding in the water.

As the bombardment ceased, the sound of the navy guns died away. The soldiers then realized that the navy, air force, and amphibious tanks had accomplished nothing. Across the water another, more terrible, sound was heard.

It was the sound of enemy guns.

▼ The battleship *Nevada* opens fire. She survived a Japanese torpedo and five bomb hits at Pearl Harbor, and was back with the fleet for D-Day.

H·HOUR / 6:30 A.M. OMAHA BEACH

Dog Green, Dog Red, and Easy Green sectors

Onshore, from high and low in the cliffs, the German gunners opened fire. The ramps of landing craft went down and Americans began to die.

Pilots desperately tried to escape the enemy crossfire. They fought, and died, to get the troops ashore anywhere they could. Combat engineers worked with tremendous courage but they could not clear obstacles in the water. The air was thick with smoke and the smell of cordite. A thousand American soldiers were caught in a deadly storm of fire and iron. Death was everywhere. Horribly wounded men screamed for help. Medical corpsmen were shot down. Men in deep shock and tears, men without equipment or weapons, struggled in the endless fire on Omaha beach.

Officers were dead, and soldiers were leaderless. The infantry was scattered in the wrong places on the long shoreline. Survivors who made it across the sand were stopped by barbed wire. Unable to move forward, the exhausted and traumatized men looked back to the water. They saw the devastating power of the German guns and knew that no one could escape alive.

The Nazis had created the closest thing to hell that American soldiers ever faced. But, here and there at small spots along the four-mile Omaha shore, the fire was less hot. It was at these places that too few soldiers must do the work of a thousand men.

SPALDING'S SOLDIERS

Easy Red sector

Bullets cracked against the boat's metal sides as it zigzagged between the obstacles. It was the only boat in sight. The landing craft scraped ground, the ramp went down, and Lt. Spalding shouted that he'd go first.

Spalding jumped into waist-deep water. His heart was racing, pounding, as he stepped forward with legs that moved slowly as in a nightmare. An artillery shell exploded somewhere close and a geyser of water sent waves up Spalding's side. The sweat on his skin turned ice-cold but he thought, *I can do this, please God, I can lead these men.* Two hundred yards of white-capped waves rose and fell to the shore of Omaha beach.

Behind him, the last soldiers jumped from the landing craft. The men spread out. It had been drilled into their heads. *If you get hit, don't take a buddy with you.* Each man struggled alone and fought to control his fear.

And then the ground disappeared.

The boat had landed on a sand bar. Before Spalding could shout a warning, the water closed over his head.

Everywhere, men were falling in the water. DiGaetano inflated his life preserver, but it was attached to the flamethrower on his back. Trapped under water, he held his breath and frantically sawed through the straps with his knife.

Reese dropped his rifle as he fought to the surface. He gasped for air and was blinded by wet toilet paper. It streamed out from under his helmet where he had put it earlier. Somehow, he didn't lose his glasses as he pulled gobs of tissue off his face.

Heavy packs and weapons pulled men under. Sims yelled, "I can't make it!" Colson shouted to him, "Dump the gun! Get in alive! Come on!"

◀ Mist and smoke hang heavy over Easy Red as the 16th Regiment lands on Omaha beach.

▲ This is the knife, with its scabbard, that saved Vinny DiGaetano's life on D-Day.

▲ Curtis Colwell was a coal miner in eastern Kentucky before Pearl Harbor. The Japanese attack made him so angry that he volunteered for the army. His wife cried the day he left. She was sure Curt would never come home to her and their young child.

▲ Bruce Buck was trained as an Army engineer and cook. Sent overseas in 1943, he was assigned instead to the 1st Division as a rifleman, and joined E Company in Sicily.

Soldiers dropped equipment to save themselves and help each other. DiGaetano saved one man and yanked him on to the floating flamethrower. Together, they used it as a raft.

Spalding lost his carbine and managed to swim. He heard Piasecki call for help, and the lieutenant and Streczyk pulled him to shallow water. There, behind obstacles of wooden stakes, some men collapsed and wretched violently, too weak to go on. But the beach was worse than the water. From all sides came the roar of guns. The soldiers were now in the middle of the enemy trap. A hundred yards ahead, barbed wire strung along a short ridge blocked the way.

Sgt. Curt Colwell and his squad made it to the wire-capped ridge. They set off bangalores and the blast added to the pounding din of gunfire. When the debris settled, there was a wide gap torn in the barbed wire. The first men rushed through.

Spalding dropped onto the ground in front of the ridge and took cover. Reese jumped over him and thought the lieutenant was dead. Bullets were whining by, some so close Spalding could feel them pass. His eyes were on the men still coming in. Everyone was too waterlogged to run and it looked like they were moving into a very strong wind.

DiGaetano sloshed out of the surf. Exhausted, he left the flamethrower bobbing on the incoming tide and flopped on to the beach. A bullet landed between his legs, sending up a little geyser of sand. Vinny stumbled to the safety of the ridge where Streczyk yelled, "Go get that flamethrower!" DiGaetano dodged bullets and staggered back with the heavy weapon.

A shell screamed down like a giant knife cutting through paper. The shell exploded and a metal fragment sliced into Pfc. Tilley's right shoulder. Sgt. Phelps picked up Tilley's BAR, and helped his friend move forward.

A bullet hit Pvt. Roper in the foot and he fell. He tried to get off his boot but his trembling hands couldn't undo the laces on his legging. Spalding helped him and Bowen gave first aid.

Beyond the wire, more than 100 yards away at the base of the slope, were demolished houses that looked like ancient ruins. The men, including the wounded, had taken cover there behind the stone walls. A field of landmines had stopped the advance. Streczyk said it couldn't be crosssed. He took Gallagher with him and went to find a way out.

Bruce Buck charged up the beach, holding his rifle in front of him. He registered the yellow blur of an enemy tracer bullet just as it struck the rifle stock above his left hand. The stock shattered, and wood and metal fragments hit his eyes. He stumbled and dropped down beside Spalding.

There was no sign of E Company. Buck painfully washed his eyes with canteen water. Spalding worked the antenna out of his radio and tried to contact Capt. Wozenski but the radio was dead. Spalding looked down and saw that the mouthpiece had been shot away. Shaken and too dazed to notice that Buck was wounded, Spalding put the useless radio back on his shoulder, and went through the gap in the barbed wire. Bowen bandaged Buck's eyes.

Spalding looked back to the beach. On the water, more boats were coming in. Some were in flames. Then, in the distance, he saw American soldiers mowed down by machine gun fire. Spalding could only watch it happen and he decided not to look back anymore.

Spalding and his men were the only soldiers off Easy Red. There were enemy gunners to the left, to the right, and up above. The men had very few grenades, no mortar; most of their heavy weapons were at the bottom of the English Channel. Some of the soldiers had no weapons at all.

Then things got worse. Out of nowhere, enemy machine gun bullets made a row of dots in a stone wall. Someone knew that invaders got ashore.

▲ Fred Reese was one of the new guys in England. During roll call, everyone found out that his first name was Elmer (his middle name was Frederick). No one would call him Fred after that. His nickname became "Little Elmo."

▼ There were no ready-made foxholes on Omaha since the air force bombers missed the beach. Evacuated houses, destroyed in the navy bombardment, gave some cover to the invading soldiers.

BREAKING THROUGH

Colson, Sims, and Ramundo spread out beside a wall at the base of the slope. Enemy rifle fire was all around and getting stronger. Colson had picked up a Browning Automatic Rifle to replace his lost mortar. He scanned the hillside for a way out. Ramundo looked back to the water. He saw soldiers trapped on the beach, far from the gap in the barbed wire.

Ramundo shouted, "I'm going to get the company!" Colson hollered back, "Don't go down there, Ramundo, stay here! They'll come through!"

But Ramundo took off. There was gunfire and Colson didn't need to look to know what happened.

On the other side of the wall, Gallagher jumped down next to Spalding. He told the lieutenant there was a path that looked okay. It was a trail through the minefield for German gunners. Krauts were all over the place. The path ran up through a gully so men would have some cover, but there were trip wires.

Spalding gave the word: *We're going up.*

Sgt. Blades, who got a bazooka ashore, went first. Behind him were Phelps, Slaydon, and Curley. Lt. Spalding was next and he kept his eyes on the crest of the slope. Behind him, he heard Sgt. Bisco keep repeating, "Lieutenant, watch the ground."

Sgt. Blades spotted an enemy gun just off the path, and he fired his bazooka and missed. The enemy gunner opened fire. A bullet struck Blades' left arm. Bullets hit Ray Curley and Joe Slaydon. Phelps moved up with the BAR and was shot in both legs.

Streczyk, Dzierga, and others rushed in from the side. A single German threw up his hands and scooted down the slope on his backside. Streczyk shouted questions in German. The enemy prisoner answered in Polish. He was one of many men from occupied countries in Hitler's Army.

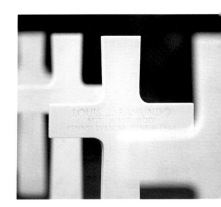

▲ Lou Ramundo was 24 years old. He fought through North Africa and Sicily, where he won a Silver Star for valor. He is buried above Easy Red.

▲ A concrete gun emplacement, usually called a pillbox, still stands on the slope above Omaha beach. The cliffs in the background separated the Americans from the British soldiers on Gold beach.

◀ An American soldier in combat.

Streczyk switched to Polish. Stan Dzierga joined in. The prisoner said there were other soldiers close by. They all loved Americans, he said. When the bombardment began, the group voted not to fight, but German sergeants made them do it.

The gunner had been alone in a one-man foxhole. Streczyk whacked the prisoner on the head and yelled, "So why are you shooting us now?" The gunner was scared and kept insisting he had not shot any Americans.

Bieder and Piasecki had gone after a second machine gun nest. Bieder launched a grenade and missed. He didn't miss the second time, and he and Piasecki brought back a prisoner. Bieder's stomach turned when he saw Ray Curley. There was a lot of blood and Wally could only think, *Well, at least you're going home, pal.*

Meanwhile, Sgt. Colson charged ahead up the path. He stopped just below the crest of the hill and motioned for Sims. Above was a pillbox. Colson saw an enemy soldier just as he tossed down a grenade. Clarence dropped to the ground and braced himself, but the German forgot to pull the pin. When the grenade didn't go off, Colson yelled for Sims to follow him with clips of fresh ammo. Then Colson leapt forward, firing the BAR from the hip.

▶ A German gunner guards the shore of Nazi Europe.

The sergeant moved and shot so fast that Sims had trouble keeping up. Colson ran through a trench, spraying bullets at the pillbox, keeping enemy soldiers away from their guns. As soon as the sergeant ran out of bullets, the private would slam in a new clip. Colson's finger never left the trigger. He got within a few short yards of the pillbox when the enemy waved a white rag on a stick and surrendered.

Prisoners were turned over to Sgt. Blades who guarded them with a trench knife. Bowen would stay with the wounded. Reese and others took their weapons and ammunition. Spalding picked up a German rifle to replace the carbine he lost in the water.

Streczyk set off a smoke flare. A column of thick yellow smoke billowed into the air. *Come and find us*, Streczyk thought. *We can't fight this war alone.*

There was now a very small crack in the fortress of Nazi Europe: one narrow, safe path led up from Omaha beach.

▲ Clarence Colson's high school picture and his army dog tags.

◀ Americans fight their way up a slope in Normandy.

OMAHA BEACH

Fox Green sector / About 8:00 a.m.

On the western end of Fox Green, the fire was very hot. And in that fire were nearly all the soldiers who should have been on Easy Red.

According to plan, nearly 400 men should have landed side by side as a fighting force. Instead most of E and F Company were scattered for 800 yards in a murderous crossfire on the wrong section of Omaha.

Scores of soldiers became casualties before they'd even left the water. Some were hit as they stopped to help the wounded. Others, a few at a time, made it to the protection of an embankment where barbed wire and machine gun fire trapped the survivors. There was no way forward and no going back. Sgt. Larry Fitzsimmons saw two men advance a few steps and get blown into the air by a land mine buried under the sand. Lt. Duckworth turned to say something to Capt. Wozenski and Duckworth was shot dead.

All around Wozenski, soldiers hugged the ground for dear life. Then through the haze, hundreds of yards to the right, the captain saw yellow smoke. Someone had made it off Omaha and was signaling them. There was a chance to get off the beach alive.

Wozenski got his men moving to the side rather than forward. He took out his trench knife and pressed it into mens' backs to see if they were still alive. If they were, Wozenski kicked them and yelled, "Let's go!" Then he stood in the open, firing with his carbine at the closest German pillbox. The machine gunners turned their fire on him as his men escaped and ran toward Easy Red. "Big" Ed was right behind them.

▲ Capt. Ed Wozenski (in a photo taken after the war) was E Company's commander. He was born in Bristol, Connecticut, the son of an Austrian mother and Polish father.

Easy Red sector

On Easy Red sector, many more soldiers had landed. They were follow-up troops to the first assault wave. Most of G Company made it off the beach. So did H Company, but they hit the minefield and lost a number of men.

The path began to draw scattered soldiers like water into a funnel. The men who landed near enough saw Americans on the slope, fighting their way up the craggy hillside. And as German prisoners were marched down the hill, the invaders saw the face of the enemy and saw that he could be beaten.

As a few men led the way, hundreds followed. But thousands more had no idea that progress was being made. Easy Red was one mile long. There was no communication. Radios were lost in

the fire-swept turf. Some of the heavy equipment was saved from the water and brought to shore at great cost. One man of the 1st Division, John Pinder, Jr., made two trips bringing radios ashore and was severely wounded both times. On his third trip carrying equipment, he was hit once again and killed.

Officers bravely rallied their men by example, and by pushing and shouting. Colonel George Taylor is remembered for yelling above the gunfire: "Two kinds of people are staying on this beach: the dead, and those who are going to die. Now let's get out of here!"

But nearly all the soldiers on Easy Red, and the whole of Omaha beach, were still trapped by the enemy's fire.

THE SHIPS

H plus three / 9:30 a.m.

The top commanders were at sea, 11 miles from shore. Information that reached them sounded like complete disaster. General Omar Bradley was commander of the U.S. First Army and he had to make a decision. Another assault by U.S. troops, on the beach code-named Utah, had landed against little enemy opposition. Follow-up soldiers bound for Omaha could be sent to Utah beach instead. But troops could not be evacuated. Without reinforcements, and a break in the deadlock, all of the troops already on Omaha would eventually be killed or taken prisoner.

The decision would haunt General Bradley for the rest of his life, but he gave the order to press on. Something had to be done to help, and Bradley called on the big guns of the navy.

◀ **Top:** General Omar Bradley (second from left) and naval commanders on D-Day. Binoculars were used to spot signals relayed from the beach.
Bottom: These soldiers are a "shore fire control party." The large radio was used to contact warships and direct their fire. The man at the far right holds a Signal Corps Radio 536. It is the same model of radio that Spalding carried onto Easy Red.

▼ Spalding's section wasn't the only group of soldiers to crack the Nazi fortress. By noon of D-Day, small numbers of men had moved inland at four points on bloody Omaha.

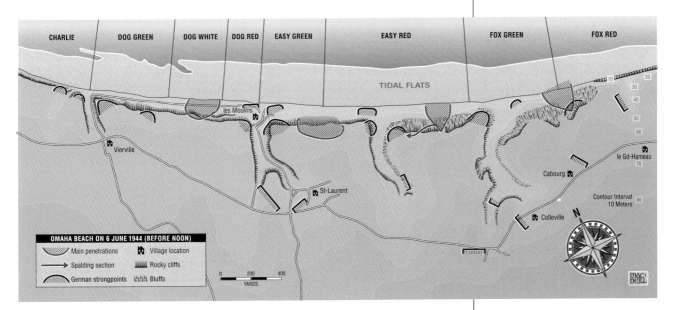

CHARLIE   DOG GREEN   DOG WHITE   DOG RED   EASY GREEN   EASY RED   FOX GREEN   FOX RED

TIDAL FLATS

les Moulins

Vierville

St-Laurent

le Gd-Hameau

Cabourg

Contour Interval
10 Meters

Colleville

OMAHA BEACH ON 6 JUNE 1944 (BEFORE NOON)
〰️ Main penetrations   Village location
→ Spalding section   Rocky cliffs
〰️ German strongpoints   Bluffs

0   200   400
YARDS

mac neil.

ATTACK

About 9:00 a.m.

How do you like the war so far, lieutenant? On top of Easy Red, Walt Bieder was watching Spalding. Bieder had seen new men crack up under enemy fire. The lieutenant was scared, so was everyone, but Spalding kept his cool and Bieder was impressed.

Spalding was thanking God for putting angels on both his shoulders. He was not only still alive; he was leading the best soldiers on earth. His daze had lifted, and Spalding now felt invincible, invulnerable. If he had said this out loud, Bieder would have said, *Enjoy the feeling while you can, sir.*

Men took turns on point, checking out suspicious areas. Streczyk and Gallagher blasted another machine gun nest and ended up with two prisoners. Sgt. Bisco went ahead and spotted a minefield. He made sure everyone knew: Don't step on patches of dead grass. That's a giveaway that Herman the German has been planting land mines. One of the soldiers seemed close to puking again. Bisco put a hand on his arm. "You're doing really good, kid," the sergeant said. "Thanks, sarge," the man croaked out and tried to make his hands stop shaking.

Then, dead ahead, Spalding saw the German strongpoint.

It was maybe 50 square yards of concrete, steel, and guns. Two big pillboxes and four concrete-and-steel shelters overlooked the beach with artillery, mortar, machine guns, and riflemen. A maze of trenches ran from one end of the strongpoint to another. The whole thing might have 40 German soldiers. Maybe more. And they were very busy firing on the beach.

The strongpoint was the company's D-Day mission. Instead of 200 men and air force bombers, Spalding had fewer than 30 men and there wasn't a bomb crater in sight. A direct assault was impossible. The attack would have to be cat-and-mouse, and Sgt. Streczyk was King Cat.

◀ German trenches above Easy Red connected underground shelters with gun positions.

▲ Pipes were used to ventilate bunkers. When Americans saw pipes like these, they knew the enemy was underground.

▲ A German soldier posed to throw a grenade. To Americans, the weapon looked like a potato masher and that's what they were called.

✪ ✪ ✪ ✪ ✪

Underground nearby, German soldiers played cards in a bunker. The men were reserves for the gun crews and waited for orders. Instead, they heard American voices just outside.

Suddenly, bullets flew into the bunker, sparking off concrete and ricocheting wildly all over the place. A voice outside yelled, in German and then in Polish, for everyone to give themselves up.

What was going on? The soldiers went to see and were taken prisoner.

✪ ✪ ✪ ✪ ✪

Sgt. Streczyk reloaded and ran into the first trench. Spalding watched the prisoners and yelled for Colson. The lieutenant still had the German rifle and decided he didn't like it. As Colson's squad came up, the lieutenant asked a man to trade weapons. The man flipped on his carbine's safety lock and traded it for the German rifle.

Enemy fire came from the left, near the road. Spalding shouted for Piasecki and Bieder to get over there.

Then everything started to happen at once.

✪ ✪ ✪ ✪ ✪

In a trench, Sgt. Streczyk was moving fast and thinking faster. Gallagher, Peterson, and others were right behind him. DiGaetano got his flamethrower roaring and sent a 15-foot flame into the gun slot of a pillbox. Smoldering Germans ran out the back and surrendered. Its fuel tanks empty, DiGaetano tossed the flamethrower aside as Streczyk swatted his back and yelled, "Good going, Dig!"

✪ ✪ ✪ ✪ ✪

In a trench in front of Spalding, 14 Germans were cornered. One of them starting tossing grenades, and then the ground began to shake.

The guns of battleships and destroyers had gone into action. Shells landed as Piasecki, Bieder, and their squad were locked in a firefight. Several Germans were shot. Others ran for the road where they were hit by the navy's fire. Few survived.

Down in a trench, Spalding made a mistake that nearly cost him his life. The lieutenant nearly stumbled on the body of a dead German and somehow couldn't believe they had killed him. Then he went around a corner and was face to face with a German rifleman. Spalding pulled the trigger of the carbine. Nothing happened. The safety was still on. Before the surprised German could react, Spalding reached for the catch but hit the ammunition clip release instead. The ammo clip clattered to the ground. Spalding turned to run but Sgt. Peterson suddenly appeared with his bazooka. The enemy soldier quickly dropped his rifle and put up his hands.

✪ ✪ ✪ ✪ ✪

Overlooking the beach from behind a steel shield, German gunners fired another shell. Seconds later it exploded hundreds of yards away and among the American troops.

The gun crew had been shooting all morning. Lifting and loading shells was hard work and they were ready for relief.

Through the drifting smoke, the Germans may have seen Wally Bieder. He aimed the grenade launcher on his rifle, and pulled the trigger.

The German gunners' work was over.

▼ German gunners fire down on the beach.

TURNING THE TIDE

11:00 a.m.

Down below on Easy Red, no one knew about the fight up above. Soldiers, engineers, and medical personnel only knew they could move without being shot. The base of the hill was crowded with troops and vehicles: tractors, tanks, bulldozers. More troops were landing. Combat engineers bulldozed paths through the dunes, loose rock, and barbed wire. Mines were cleared and anti-tank ditches were filled.

Doctors set up an aid station near the ruined house where Spalding had landed. Bowen helped get the wounded men down the slope. Buck, Slaydon, Curley, and the others were given treatment.

By 11:00 a.m., General Bradley received the first encouraging reports. One read: "Men advancing up slope behind Easy Red. Men believed ours on skyline."

◀ **Top:** Wounded American soldiers of the 16th Regiment on Easy Red. **Center:** Civilians, including children, were often caught in the crossfire of war. **Bottom:** German prisoners carry their wounded on a stretcher. Without helmets, the soldiers look like non-combatants which is exactly what prisoners of war are. Surrendering soldiers had to remove their helmets or they were considered armed (although, for some reason, one German soldier in this photo still has his helmet.)

▼ Prisoners march to the beach under guard. An American soldier, his back to the camera, is at the far right.

COLLEVILLE

Sgt. Streczyk saw Capt. Wozenski and about ten other soldiers coming up the slope. Grinning from ear to ear, he ran down to meet them and stepped square on a landmine.

Wozenski froze but nothing happened. Streczyk said, "It didn't go off on my way up either."

At the strongpoint, Spalding set off a smoke flare to warn the navy gunners. Huge shells were passing over Spalding's head like airborne jeeps and sooner or later one was bound to fall on top of his men. Twenty German prisoners stood in a group. Most were scared. One was an arrogant Nazi who kept sneering. Another German had escaped and was trying to be a sniper. He was a very bad shot and kept hitting the trees.

Wally Bieder marched the prisoners down to the beach just as Capt. Wozenski and other soldiers of E Company were coming up. When Bieder returned, he heard Spalding telling the section to move out. Captain's orders. The small village of Colleville, above Fox Green, had been captured by G Company. Now the Germans were trying to take the village back. Spalding's soldiers were to join the fight.

Spalding picked up more men on the march. They were strays from battered units including a medic, Pvt. Jessie Hamilton. DiGaetano stuck close to Reese. Vinny didn't have a weapon. Reese had a rifle and Streczyk told them to share.

Outside Colleville, the men took up positions along hedgerows, blocking a lane into town. Confused Germans were swarming all over. Confused and cautious, too cautious to use a road.

DiGaetano peered through the brush, and thought he saw a

▲ A road sign today points to Colleville.

▲ Tall hedgerows surrounded farmer's fields, and gave protection to German soldiers throughout Normandy.

◀ The church in Colleville, hit by fire from the navy warships.

▲ Vinny DiGaetano as a sergeant in 1945.

German creeping toward them in the field. Vinny nudged Reese and said, "Hey, Elmo, I see something." Reese handed over the rifle. DiGaetano took aim just as an enemy soldier saw him. As had happened to Buck, there was a loud *b-r-r-r-t-t-t* as enemy machine gun bullets ripped apart the rifle's wooden stock. It turned to splinters in Vinny's hands. A grenade sailed through the brush and exploded. A hot metal fragment tore into DiGaetano's thigh.

The men fired wildly and kept the Germans back. Jesse Hamilton crawled over and told DiGaetano to go down to the beach for a doctor. Vinny refused, he would never go back there again. The grenade fragment wasn't in very deep, and Hamilton cut it out with a knife. DiGaetano bit a stick to keep from hollering. The worst part wasn't the pain; it was having his pants around his ankles. Word quickly spread and guys started laughing and saying "Diggy" got hit in the butt. Someone said it was too big for the Germans to miss.

Very funny, guys, DiGaetano thought.

There were hundreds of metal and wood splinters in Vinny's face, hands, and arms. The medic pulled the worst of them as best he could.

The rifle gone, Reese decided he'd get something to eat. He opened a ration can just as enemy bullets hit the hedgerow, showering dirt, leaves, and twigs over him and his meat and vegetables. He tossed the can aside.

Enemy fire was coming from all directions. Friendly fire was falling too. Navy shells were hitting Colleville. Through the smoky haze, Spalding saw a runner darting toward their position. He was an American, bringing a message, but the enemy shot him down.

Then they got Fred Bisco and he never saw it coming. He was moving behind some brush and lifted his head at just the wrong moment. There was a horrible fusillade as Bisco tumbled down dead and all his friends, everyone, shot back in rage at an enemy no one could see.

The soldiers held their ground into the evening. They had help, without knowing it, from their allies. The British and Canadian assaults drew enemy counterattacks miles away from Omaha beach. If the Germans hit Colleville in force, Spalding's men and other Americans would have been swatted aside and the village recaptured. Instead, our allies chewed the German counterattacks to pieces.

Along the hedgerows, around 8:00 p.m., the ammunition was nearly gone. When Spalding was down to his last six bullets, he organized a retreat. One by one, everyone crawled along the ditch until they reached the makeshift company command post.

Soldiers looked around for buddies, and wondered where everyone was. Then Capt. Wozenski was heard to cry out in angry grief, "Where are my men? Where was the support we were promised?"

At that moment, the terrible cost of D-Day was bitter as defeat. Spalding thought of Ramundo and Bisco. He tried to push it from his mind and focused on the fact that he had done his job.

Streczyk made the rounds, checking on men whose day began 18 hours ago. Some soldiers would keep watch while others tried to get some rest.

Medics asked men for their blankets to keep the wounded men warm on the beach. Fred Reese scrounged some food. The breakfast that morning of a salami sandwich, apple, and coffee seemed like a different lifetime. As Reese drifted to a restless sleep in a fox hole he was thinking, *All the jobs in the Army and I had to get one where I get shot at. Here we go. . . .*

Daylight would bring another day of war.

▲ Fred Bisco was 28 years old. He was drafted on 7 August 1941 and shipped overseas with the 1st Division in July 1942. Bisco fought in North Africa and Sicily before landing, for his last day on earth, in Normandy. His family had his body sent home for burial in North Arlington, New Jersey.

On D-Day

On D-Day the Allies pushed the enemy off the edge of Nazi Europe. On Omaha beach, no single group did more for victory than John Spalding and his men. It seems like a miracle. Their day began in the middle of the night with three hours of throwing up on each other until they left the landing craft and nearly drowned. Then they staggered to shore, some without weapons, to take on the German Army. Yet Spalding's men were the first to take prisoners, first on top of the hill, first to clear a way forward.

Back home in the States, President Franklin Roosevelt told our nation that the invasion had succeeded. And then he said a prayer. Here are excerpts.

Almighty God, our sons, pride of our nation,
this day have set upon a mighty endeavor.

They will need Thy blessings. Their road will be long and hard,
by night and by day, without rest until the victory is won.
The darkness will be rent by noise and flame.
Men's souls will be shaken with the violences of war.

For these men are lately drawn from the ways of peace. . . . They yearn
but for the end of battle, for their return to the haven of home.

Some will never return. Embrace these, Father, and receive them,
Thy heroic servants, into Thy kingdom.

And, O Lord, give us faith. Give us faith in Thee; Faith in our sons;
Faith in each other; Faith in our united crusade.

▶ On 7 June, the U.S. 2nd Division was photographed coming ashore. Grass-fires and bulldozers had already changed the landscape. The soldiers are marching up from Easy Red, directly toward the spot where Spalding and his men took out the German strongpoint.

TILL VICTORY

In March 1945, four and a half million Allied soldiers struck the Nazi heartland. They had crossed the Rhine River to finish the job begun on D-Day.

June and July 1944 had been spent blasting through Normandy, hedgerow by hedgerow. Then came August and the great Allied breakout. The enemy was chased from France and, by mid-September, the 1st Division stood on Germany's border. The country's great river, a barrier that protected its heart for centuries, lay 50 miles away. But the enemy recovered its strength as they defended their homeland. Autumn rain turned to winter snow as the Americans were battered to a stalemate. On 16 December, the German Army launched a major offensive and smashed through the American line. In a great winter battle, the attack was stopped as a salient, or "Bulge." The enemy was defeated, the Bulge was flattened, and by 2 February, the 1st Division was on German soil and fighting to the Rhine.

The casualties, and flow of replacements, never stopped. Replacements weren't only needed for battle casualties. No person can long endure the horrors of war. The U.S. Surgeon General warned that the maximum combat the human mind and spirit can withstand was 200 days. Most men broke much sooner.

The 1st Division was in combat for 443 days from North Africa to the end. From D-Day alone, the division suffered 15,000 men killed, wounded, missing in action; and 14,000 nonbattle casualties in the soul-shattering inferno of war.

That was the price for freeing the world. On 8 May 1945, Berlin had fallen and Germany surrendered. The Nazi government, enemy of human life and freedom, had been wiped from the face of the earth.

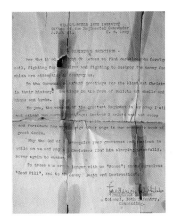

▲ During the Battle of the Bulge, soldiers of the 16th Regiment received this message from their commander: "For the third straight Christmas we find ourselves on foreign soil and fighting to destroy the enemy forces which are attempting to destroy us.... May the God of War recognize your greatness and continue to smile on us and may next Christmas find him sleeping peacefully, never again to awaken. To those who are no longer with us 'Peace'; among ourselves 'Good Will'; and to the enemy 'Death and Destruction.'"

◄ In April 1945, American soldiers move through a devastated German city. Nazi dictator Adolf Hitler would not surrender even when he knew the war was lost. He turned his insane rage against the German people and wanted them to suffer for losing his war.

John Spalding

was awarded the Distinguished Service Cross for valor. After D-Day, decimated units were combined and rebuilt. Spalding's section became a rifle platoon which he led until 27 September. On that day, he was wounded by enemy artillery. Spalding was patched up, assigned a new platoon, and his D-Day soldiers never saw him again. During the winter Battle of the Bulge, the strain of command grew worse and worse. John became indecisive, afraid the wrong decision would get one of his men killed. At night he had nightmares, battle dreams, until he stopped sleeping altogether. In February, Spalding was in such awful shape that he could not go on. He was evacuated to the United States with a severe respiratory infection and combat exhaustion. The Army wanted Spalding to train troops but he refused because he now had an intense hatred of guns. After the war and his discharge from service, John entered politics and was elected to the House of Representatives. He died in 1959.

▶ Seven men in Lt. Spalding's section received the Distinguished Service Cross. The men were John Spalding, George Bowen, Richard Gallagher, Ken Peterson, Curt Colwell, Clarence Colson, and Phil Streczyk. Photographers took pictures: Newspaper stories would appear in hometown papers. Stan Dzierga and Walt Bieder both had been promoted to sergeant and were awarded Silver Stars. After brief ceremonies, each soldier took off his medal and went back to the frontline.

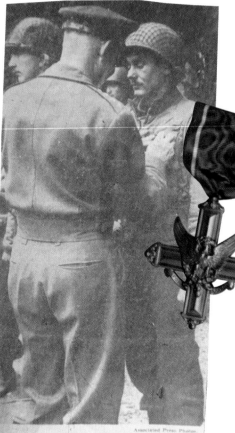

Associated Press Photo

PLEASURE'S ALL "IKE'S," 'TWOULD SEEM from outsized smile edging back along General Eisenhower's cheek as he pins the D.S.C. on Second Lt. John N. Spaulding, of Owensboro, Ky., who receives it in deadly serious modesty.

▶ John Spalding's granddaughter, Tina, kneels by his grave in Owensboro, Kentucky. Photo inset: Spalding shortly after the war.

Joe Slaydon recovered from his wounds on D-Day and rejoined E Company. On 20 November 1944, during a German counterattack in the Hürtgen forest, he was badly wounded a second time. No longer able to be a soldier, Slaydon was sent home and discharged. He died in North Carolina in 1969.

Bruce Buck spent two months healing after D-Day before being sent back to the frontline. He was platoon runner during the fierce battle of Aachen. "I was the one Streczyk always sent back to the command post for ammunition," Bruce remembers. "I would load as many bandoliers of ammo as I could carry around my neck and shoulders. Then I'd run from the command post up the hill. There was an open space, and the Germans would shoot the heck out of everything, trying to shoot me. And I just had to make a run for it, that's all I could do. I got the Silver Star out of that deal." He stayed in Germany as part of the occupation forces until his discharge in October 1945.

Stan Dzierga got a package when he was in basic training. It was from a girl named Fran, a friend of a friend, and inside was a box of cookies and a wallet. Stan was carrying the wallet and a prayer book in his breast pocket when he was hit with a piece of shrapnel. It went through the book, but the wallet stopped the chunk of metal before it reached Stan's chest. A later injury took Stan out of combat, and he was assigned to duty in France where he trained cooks and clerks to be riflemen. Stan and Fran corresponded throughout the war and were married when Stan came home.

▶ Stan Dzeriga today.

Phil Streczyk

disappeared one day in Belgium—but not for long. On 2 August 1944, the 1st Division advanced so quickly that it collided with a retreating German Army. During the wild fight, Stan Dzierga saw an armored gun clanking straight for him. Dzierga screamed a warning and was about to shoot when the driver waved and yelled, "Hiya, Stan!" It was Streczyk herding prisoners to the American lines. No one ever thought Phil Streczyk was afraid or had a breaking point, but his end came in the Hürtgen forest. Through thick mud and miserably cold rain, the 16th Regiment attacked through minefields and under artillery that burst in the treetops. The air was filled with lethal shell fragments and tree limbs that could smash a man like a club, or pierce flesh like a spear. Dick Gallagher and many others were killed in the endless firestorms. In four days, around mid-November, the regiment advanced just two miles at a cost of 1,000 casualties. As shells were exploding, Streczyk suddenly shouted words that no one could understand. His body shook uncontrollably as Curt Colwell and others grabbed their great friend and hugged him to the ground until they could get him away to safety. He was evacuated to a hospital in the states. Phil slowly recovered, but battle dreams and painful wounds were now part of his life. Streczyk became a builder, moved to Florida, and raised a family. He died in 1957.

▶ Capt. Wozenski congratulates Phil Streczyk on his medal for valor. His family had moved to New York so he was now a New York City hero. At right, Streczyk is with his wife and children on a beach in St. Petersburg, Florida.

NEW YORK CITY WAR HEROES DECORATED IN FRANCE

Sgt. Phillip Streczyk is congratulated by his company commander after receiving the Distinguished Service Cross from Gen. Dwight D. Eisenhower.

Sgt. Lawrence J. Fitzsimmons is greeted by his company commander after the General pinned the Distinguished Service Cross on him.

Associated Press

Curt Colwell

took over the platoon after Streczyk was gone. Later, Colwell was wounded and Wally Bieder took over from him. Curt went back to coal mining after the war. About all he ever said about it was, "We slept on the ground and we ate when we could." His wife could only cry with joy that he came home. The family went to church and, when they returned, someone had stolen Curt's medals.

Ed Wozenski

devoted his life to serving his country. He retired from the Army as a brigadier general in 1972 with two Distinguished Service Crosses, two Silver Stars, and numerous other medals from the United States, Belgium, and France. Everything about "Big" Ed, including his wisdom and compassion, was larger than life. His tremendous energy came from something his father told him just before he passed away: "There are so many more things to be done." For Wozenski, that phrase became a credo to live by. Just before Ed's own death in 1987, he said those same words to his brother Joe. Then Ed added that he was at peace with God.

◀ Plaques honoring Ed Wozenski are unveiled at the Bristol Armory in 1988. An army officer stands next to Wozenski's granddaughter, Laura.

Clarence Colson

saw more than 400 days in the dust of Algeria and Tunisia; the ravines of Sicily; across France, Belgium, and deep into Germany. When the war was over, he just wanted to get back to his family's farm and forget it ever happened. He married the girl who lived down the hill and never told her or anyone else about the war. His few good memories were of liberated villages where joyful people hugged and kissed the marching soldiers, of Capt. Wozenski, and their mess sergeant, Eddie Vaughn, who drove through enemy fire to deliver their Thanksgiving dinner. It was a cold turkey sandwich and cold coffee, but no food ever tasted better. But most memories still bring pain, He never could forget how Lou Ramundo was shot, or the day in November 1944 when an enemy mortar shell hit Richard Sims. Clarence recalls, "We just got dug in and a shell exploded. I hollered to him. He didn't respond. So I jumped over to his foxhole to check and I said, 'Sims! Are you all right?' Then I saw that he was hit and he was dead."

Sergeant Clarence (NMI) Colson, 12022782, 16th In   United States Army, for extraordinary heroism in action against the enem   1944, in France. When the landing craft carrying Sergeant Colson a   d grounded some 400 yards offshore, the men were forced to   under heavy enemy machine gun fire. Sergeant Colson, despite   moved from one man to another encouraging and aiding them shore   g shore, Sergeant Colson was determined to continue the atta   moved across the fire swept beach, locating and organizing his s   ion. He then took   ng position in clear view of the en   cted his fi   chine gun emplacement while s   men cut a gap in   advanced, Sergeant Co   squad through an   assault the enemy mac   pite enemy hand   Sergeant Colson reached   the gun position his rifle blazing. In   tion against   ant Colson killed sever   y and forced the   The courage, initiative   exhibited by great credit on hims   ing with the   Armed Forces. Enter   litary service from New York.

Cattaraugus Sergeant Is Honored

IN FRANCE, Oct. 8.—Maj. Gen. Joseph L. Collins congratulates Sgt. Clarence Colson of Cattaraugus, N. Y., who has just been decorated with the DSC.

◄ At left, Clarence Colson being awarded the DSC for valor. His charge up the slope was one of the bravest acts on D-Day. Above, his citation and medal. At right, Clarence Colson today.

Ken Peterson

came home after the war with the Silver Star, Bronze Star, Distinguished Service Cross, and Purple Heart. He was wounded during the Bulge, treated, and sent back to Germany where he was wounded a second time. "Pete" joined Passaic's fire department and retired as chief in 1990. He died at New Jersey's State Fireman's Home in 1998.

Fred Reese

couldn't believe his eyes. It was early 1945, and there stood Ray Curley. He had sneaked out of a hospital in England and hitched rides across Europe to find E Company.

"What are you doing?" Reese said. "I thought you were home already!"

"Nah," Curley said. "I wanted to be with you guys." They would wish he hadn't.

Across the Rhine River, on 30 March, while running down an alley in some German town, Ray Curley was machine-gunned in the back and killed. Reese tried to get the gunner, but was badly shot up himself. Evacuated to a hospital in the states, Fred was home on leave on 14 August 1945. He was walking to a grocery store with his parents when two 12-year-old girls ran up to Fred and thew handfuls of rice in his face. That's how he learned that Japan had surrendered and World War II was over.

▶ Fred Reese today.

▼ 1st Division soldiers rest against a wall in Germany. The words read, "We are victorious because we believe in Adolf Hitler and his Great German Empire." The soldiers might have added, *"Nicht."*

Vinny DiGaetano

worried his family. They received a telegram, just a few days before Germany surrendered, saying he was wounded in action. Weeks passed with no letter from him. His sister contacted the Red Cross and an Army chaplain tracked DiGaetano down. Vinny had been hit by a Screaming Meemie, German mortar that screamed through the air and then went silent just before it exploded. The blast blew DiGaetano four feet in the air and he landed deafened and paralyzed. As Vinny recovered in a hospital the Army told him he was shipping out soon for the invasion of Japan. By the time the chaplain showed up, Vinny didn't care who was worried about him. He had been wounded four times in the war, and he knew he'd never survive another day of combat. Then word came that there would be no invasion. The U.S. had dropped a new weapon, the atomic bomb, and Japan had surrendered. Vinny came home a changed man. A cousin who served in the Signal Corps dropped by one night. He had made recordings of Screaming Meemies and he played the tape at a family gathering. Vinny went beserk at the sound and he had to be restrained from tossing the cousin out the window. Word got around that Vinny was nuts. His girlfriend married him anyway. Then she woke up screaming one night because Vinny, in his sleep, had his hands around her throat. DiGaetano began seeing a psychiatrist and it helped him find peace. Having survived World War II, he now takes every day as a gift.

▼ Below, military police of the Red One flank the division's 100,000th POW in April 1945. Right, DiGaetano today.

Walt Bieder

was never wounded and never missed a day's combat from Sicily to German-occupied Czechoslovakia. There, in May 1945, the 1st Division linked up with our Russian ally advancing from the east. The Russians were so impressed with Bieder's endurance that they gave him a medal. "I nearly cracked one time but I caught myself," he says. "I was sitting in a foxhole and we were getting shelled. I started to shake and I just said 'STOP!' and I got hold of myself quick. I don't know how I did it. When you get shelled day after day, it kind of gets you." After Germany surrendered, Walt had enough service "points" (under a complex Army system) to go home. Like most returning soldiers, Bieder felt out of place in his own hometown. Few people understood what soldiers had suffered. Walt was on the street on 14 August 1945 when everyone just went wild. Japan had surrendered and the whole city began to party. Bieder never once lost control in combat, but he lost it now. He started crying and screaming, "Fools! Get down on your knees and thank God! Thank the boys who did it and say a prayer for the ones who aren't coming back!" Today, Walt lives near Washington, D.C., and a memorial to the honored dead of the 1st Division. Walt has only been there twice because the memory of fallen buddies is almost too much to bear.

"So many names," he says, "so many good men."

They won the victory and saved the world. Let us respect that gift and live our lives with honor.

Home Town Hero

WHEN a numerically superior enemy force attacked his company, Sergeant Walter R. Bieder advanced to an exposed vantage point and with effective rifle fire assisted in disabling numerous enemy vehicles and in repelling the enemy.

Sergeant Bieder, 24, was awarded the Bronze Star Medal for this heroic action in Belgium last September. The infantryman has been overseas since April, 1943. His mother, Mrs. Martha Bieder, lives at 1804 Tarlton Ave.

A WORLD WAR II CHRONOLOGY

The Road to War: 1918-1939

11 November 1918

The First World War ended with Germany's defeat. Many Germans blamed their political leaders. Among them was an angry and self-pitying soldier named Adolf Hitler. He would preach hatred and violence and ultimately lead his nation to war once again.

6 November 1932

GERMANY: Hitler's followers, the Nazi political party, grew in strength during the worldwide economic depression. No single political party was more popular. In the 1932 election, the Nazis got a third of the vote. One third was enough to bring the Nazis to power. And Hitler soon seized the powers of a dictator.

1936-1938

GERMANY: Hitler and Italy's dictator, Benito Mussolini, signed a pact for a Rome-Berlin "axis of power." Japan later became a third member of the Axis.

In 1938, the German army was on the march. The Nazis occupied Austria in May. Czechoslovakia was taken the next year. Germany's old enemies, Britain and France, warned that another act of aggression would mean war.

1 September 1939

POLAND: More than a million German soldiers moved across the border into Poland. And Europe was at war.

Blitzkreig (Lightning War): 1939-1941

27 September 1939

Poland was conquered before the democracies could intervene. An evil Nazi regime took control and enslaved the conquered people. Nearly five and a half million Slavic men, women, and children would die in Poland. Three million were Jews.

April-June 1940

NORTHERN EUROPE: France, Britain, Australia, New Zealand, and Canada declared war on Germany (the United States declared neutrality).

▲ Adolf Hitler at a Nazi party rally in 1928.

▼ German stormtroopers race past a burning building. Hitler's army invaded Poland from the west while Josef Stalin's Russian army invaded from the east. Poland was crushed and surrendered on 6 October 1939.

▲ The Battle of Britain raged from 10 July to 30 October 1940. More than 35,000 civilians were killed or injured in those months, including 5,000 children.

▼ There was much for the German army to celebrate from October 1939 through November 1941. But, in Russia, Josef Stalin signaled the party's end by declaring, "If they want a war of extermination, they shall have one." He kept his word.

But Germany's enemies were far away and unprepared for warfare. Nothing could stop Germany's advance. In April 1940, the Nazis smashed Norway and Denmark. In early May, the German army crossed the border for Belgium, Holland, Luxembourg, and France. British and French forces were pushed to the sea at Dunkirk and evacuated to England. France surrendered in June (and her new government, in Vichy, put France on a road of collaboration with the Nazis).

Most of Europe was now under Nazi rule. Hitler gave Britain a choice: surrender or die. But British Prime Minister Winston Churchill was defiant: "We shall defend our island, whatever the cost may be. We shall fight on the beaches . . . we shall fight in the fields and in the streets . . . we shall never surrender!"

10 July 1940

ENGLAND: German bombers struck English towns. Britain's Royal Air Force (strengthened by pilots from Poland, Canada, and Czechoslavokia) struck back. The Battle of Britain had begun, and by October, Hitler faced his first defeat. The RAF slowly tore the German air force apart. Britain had won the battle, but German bombs still blasted England in bomb raids known as the Blitz.

Meanwhile, Mussolini was in trouble. He had tried, and failed, to imitate Hitler's success. The Italians bungled an invasion of Greece, and the Greek army tossed them back. Then the Italians attacked Egypt, and were forced to retreat back to their colony of Libya. Hitler sent his army to Mussolini's rescue.

April 1941

The German army sliced through Yugoslavia and Greece. In North Africa, German forces pushed the British back to Egypt. With Mussolini propped up, Hitler could now finish plans for his next invasion.

Russia had fought Germany in the First World War until the Russian czar was overthown in a revolution. In 1917, Russia became the Soviet Union with Josef Stalin as dictator. It was this vast, resource-rich country that Hitler planned to strike.

22 June 1941

RUSSIA: Exactly one year after conquering France, 3.6 million Axis soldiers crossed the Russian border and began a war of terrorism. German soldiers were pardoned in advance for the murder of civilians. It was evil and stupid. The Nazis might have conquered the Soviet Union had they liberated the people from Communism. Instead, the brutalized Russians rose up in a Patriotic War for survival.

Germany wasn't alone in the attack. Finland, Romania, Bulgaria, Hungary, and Italy also declared war on Russia. The Nazis believed this combined force could conquer the Soviet Union before winter. For a time, it seemed they were right.

By September, the Axis decimated the Red Army and conquered the Ukraine and the Crimean peninsula. In October, Hitler was claiming victory. But a month later, his troops were stuck in the mud as the rain of autumn fell. Then rain turned to snow. Hitler began saying that Blitzkreig was a stupid word; no one should expect a quick victory. By December, the invaders were stuck 18 miles from Moscow, freezing in the cold.

7 December 1941

HAWAII: Japan was ready to enter the war. In a surprise attack, Japanese bombers struck the American naval base at Pearl Harbor, Hawaii. This wasn't all. At the same time, Japanese forces attacked the Dutch East Indies; the British in Malaya; and the Americans in the Philippines, Guam, Wake, and Midway.

The United States was now in the fight. The United States, Russia, Britain, Canada, Mexico, and 21 other nations and governments-in-exile around the world became the Allies. Calling themselves "The United Nations," these 26 countries pledged "to ensure life, liberty, independence, and religious freedom, and to preserve the rights of man and justice." To do so, the war had to be won.

January-August 1942

UNITED STATES: Germany struck America in the only way she could. Her bombers could not reach America, but U-Boats (German submarines) could sink our ships. The coastal waters of the United States were the most dangerous in all the world.

On the other side of the globe, in May, the Japanese drive to Australia and New Zealand was halted at the Battle of the Coral Sea. A month later, at Midway, American divebombers sank the Japanese carrier fleet that had attacked Pearl Harbor. Meanwhile, Japanese forces landed, and were stranded, on two of Alaska's Aleutian islands. In the Pacific and the China Sea, Japan went on the defensive, and the U.S. went on the attack. The offensive began on 7 August 1942 when the U.S. Marines landed on Guadalcanal, an island east of New Guinea. It was a fierce fight on land and sea that lasted until 9 February 1943. By that time, Americans were battling Hitler's forces in North Africa.

▼ Victorious Japanese soldiers on the Philippine Islands. Despite the warning of Pearl Harbor, Americans were caught by surprise. On 8 December, the Japanese easily destroyed the grounded U.S. Far East Air Force and landed an invasion. After six months of desperate battle, the Philippines fell on 9 June 1942.

ARCTIC OCEAN

Leptev Sea

Chukchi Sea

Beaufort Sea

RUSSIA

Bering Sea

Gulf of Alaska

CANADA

Sea of Okhotsk

ALEUTIAN ISLANDS

PACIFIC

Ulaanbaatar •
MONGOLIA

MANCHURIA

Sea of Japan

Peking •

KOREA
Seoul •
HIROSHIMA

CHINA

JAPAN

TOKYO

UNITED
OF AM

Yellow Sea

• NAGASAKI

East China Sea

• OKINAWA

MIDWAY

BURMA

Canton
Hong Kong •

TAIWAN

• IWO JIMA

South China Sea

HAWAIIAN
ISLANDS

MEXIC

THAILAND

• Manila

WAKE

Pearl Harbor •

MARIANA ISLANDS

FRENCH
INDOCHINA

PHILIPPINES
Leyte Gulf

GUAM

MARSHALL ISLANDS

N. BORNEO

MALAYA

SARAWAK

CAROLINE ISLANDS

OCEAN

Singapore

GILBERT ISLANDS

EQUATOR

DUTCH EAST INDIES

N.E.
NEW
GUINEA

NEW
GUINEA

SOLOMON ISLANDS

PAPUA
TERRITORY

GUADALCANAL

Coral Sea

AUSTRALIA

Tasman Sea

Canberra

NEW ZEALAND

THE WORLD AT WAR: *1 NOVEMBER 1942*

Allied controlled

Axis controlled *(including Vichy France)*

Neutral countries

Areas of major German submarine
attacks *(7 December 1941 to 1 August 1942)*

Atlantic Ocean battlefield and
Pacific Ocean controlled by Japan

Major land conflicts before the
North African invasion

Border and country names are pre-war

▲ Through hard experience, the British armed forces in North Africa were a well-honed fighting machine. Not so the American army. U.S. forces were badly trounced by German armor at Kasserine Pass, Tunisia on 20 February 1943. From this poor showing, Germans thought the U.S. was the Allies' weak link—and they continued to believe this until 16 December 1944.

▼ Russians attack in a snowstorm. In 1943, Stalin's army ended German victories on the eastern front. Germany, on every battlefront, then fought on the defensive with far too much territory to actually defend. Hitler's response was an order of "no retreat." This doomed his army to complete destruction.

The Tide Turns: 1942-1944

23 October 1942

EGYPT: It had been 18 months since Hitler sent his tanks to prop up the Italian army. For all those months, Axis and British forces chased each other back and forth across the deserts of North Africa. Finally, on 23 October, the British "Desert Rats" won a decisive victory at the battle of El Alamein, Egypt. Axis forces retreated to Libya on 4 November. Four days later, an invasion landed behind them in the west.

8 November 1942

ALGERIA: American and British forces invaded northwest Africa in Morocco and Algeria. The main Axis army was surrounded. In May 1943, after brutal warfare in the desert sand, North Africa was won.

2 February 1943

RUSSIA: Stalingrad was one of the war's most important battles. In that ravaged city, the Nazi advance was finally stopped. The German loss at Stalingrad was enormous: 160,000 German soldiers were dead from combat and frostbite. The surviving force of 100,000 Germans in the rubble of the city finally surrendered.

19 April 1943

POLAND: The Nazi's war against conquered people went on. In the Warsaw ghetto, Jews fought back with what little weapons they had. The uprising was smashed on 13 May. The Warsaw ghetto was destroyed and its 56,000 Jews perished.

10 July 1943

ITALY: The Allies invaded Sicily (the island was liberated on 17 August).

3 September 1943

ITALY: British forces invaded mainland Italy at Reggio Calabria. The next day, Italy surrendered, but Hitler poured German troops into the country to continue the fight. Meanwhile, on the Russian front, the Soviets had launched a major attack at Kursk.

9 September 1943

ITALY: American forces (which included 25,000 soldiers from Brazil) landed on the Italian coast at Salerno. On 1 October, Naples was liberated but progress up the Italian boot was painfully slow. The Allies tried to leap ahead with an amphibious assault at Anzio. The gamble failed. Troops landed on 22 January, but the Germans kept them trapped in the beach-head until 23 May 1944.

6 June 1944
FRANCE: Allied forces invaded Nazi Europe on a 50-mile front in Normandy, France. On D-Day, more than 150,000 troops were landed, and the Allies took 10,000 casualties (both numbers are estimates, exact numbers will never be known). The worst fighting was on Omaha beach where the 1st Division's 16th Regiment advanced a mile and a half from the shore.

22 June 1944
RUSSIA: Three years to the day from Germany's surprise attack, Soviets launched a major offensive. Its aim was to clear the last of German troops from Russian soil.

20 July 1944
GERMANY: Military officers attempted to assassinate Hitler by planting a bomb. The attempt failed and Hitler was only wounded.

25 July 1944
FRANCE: The Allies had been penned in Normandy since D-Day. U.S. forces launched a massive breakout assault. Three days later, a hole had been punched through the German lines. Then, miles to the east, the Canadian army launched a second breakout. It was now the German army's turn to be on the receiving end of an Allied *Blitzkreig*.

14-15 August 1944
SOUTHERN FRANCE: American and Free French forces invade the French Mediterranean..

25 August 1944
FRANCE: The Allies liberated Paris. Retreating Germans raced for home: the fortifications known as the West Wall (or Siegfried Line) that protected the German frontier.

14 September 1944
THE HÜRTGEN FOREST: U.S. troops entered the Hürtgen forest. Savage fighting there would go on until 8 December.

15 September 1944
NORTHWEST EUROPE: The Allied Blitz came to an end against German fortifications. Hitler now planned an attack that was Germany's last chance for victory.

▲ A British soldier rescues a dog from the wreckage of what once was a house.

▼ A Frenchwoman welcomes an American soldier.

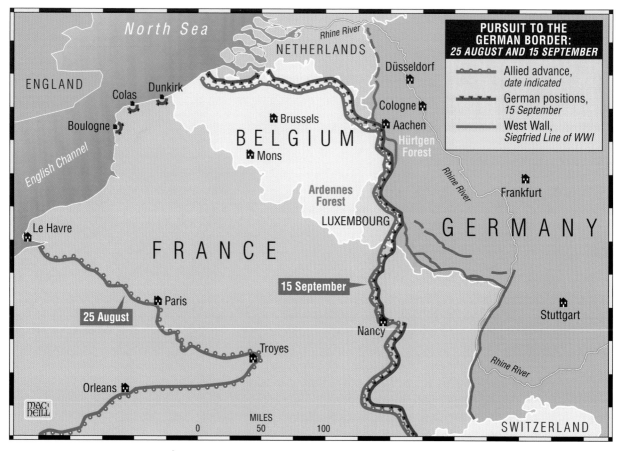

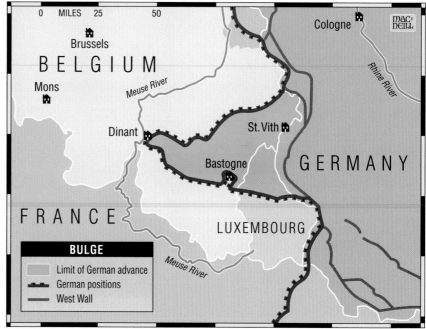

▶ The Battle of the Bulge was Hitler's last, desperate, attempt to win the war. Instead, it was the U.S. Army's greatest victory. The map at left show the limit of the German advance—far from their goal of the North Sea. This would have driven a wedge between the Americans and our British and Canadian allies fighting to the north.

16 December 1944

THE ARDENNES, BELGIUM: The German attack began. It was aimed at what Hitler believed was the weak point: the front held by American soldiers. Instead, the outnumbered Americans fought with incredible bravery. The Germans got no further than a 45-mile penetration (or "Bulge") into the American lines.

Year of Victory: 1945

16 January 1945

THE ARDENNES, BELGIUM: Americans had flattened the "Bulge" and pushed the Germans back to their West Wall.

4 February 1945

YALTA, UKRAINE, THE CRIMEA: Leaders of "The Big Three" (Roosevelt, Churchill, and Stalin) met and reached accord on the post-war world. Among other points, Stalin agreed to allow free elections in Poland—a point he later would not honor. Central Europe would be liberated from the Nazis only to be enslaved by communism. Hitler's war, aimed in part at the destruction of Russia, resulted instead in the spread of communism throughout the world.

8 February 1945

THE RHINELAND: Allies pushed forward and entered Germany's Rhineland region. By the third week of March, the Allies were crossing at many points along the Rhine River. In April, the Allied forces were spreading everywhere across Germany while Hitler was sending orders to armies that no longer existed.

23 April 1945

GERMANY: U.S. and Russian troops met at Germany's Elbe River. It was the first junction of the Allies fighting from east and west. General Hodges, of the U.S. First Army, asked for instructions from U.S. headquarters. Hodges received a message that said: "Be nice to them." In 1944 and early 1945, the Russians had knocked four of Hitler's allies out of the war: Finland, Romania, Hungary, and Bulgaria had all changed sides and declared war on Germany. In January 1945, the Russians captured Warsaw, Poland, and advanced into East Germany. There, the Soviets committed widespread acts of brutality and murder as they sought vengeance on German people. By 26 April, the Russians began their assault on Hitler's capital, Berlin.

▲ A wounded German is patched up by an American medic.

▼ Winston Churchill, Franklin D. Roosevelt, and Josef Stalin at the Yalta Conference.

▲ A German officer (eating an American soldier's rations) in the ruins of his country.

▼ Liberated from a concentration camp, these refugees are going to build a new nation. They hold the symbol of Zion which will soon become the flag of Israel.

28 April 1945
ITALY: Mussolini was executed by Italian enemies of his Fascist regime.

30 April 1945
GERMANY: Hitler committed suicide with Russian troops just a quarter of a mile away from his headquarters.

7 May 1945
A shattered Germany surrendered. The war in Europe was over.

21 June 1945
OKINAWA: Fighting ended on Okinawa, an island 350 miles southwest of Japan. There had been no pause in the war against Japan. The Army Air Force had firebombed her cities. Ground forces had leapfrogged island chains, pushed across New Guinea, and reclaimed the Philippines. Americans heard for the first time of specks on the map such as Saipan, Guam, and Iwo Jima. Now an invasion of the Japanese homeland was scheduled for 1 November.

16 July 1945
NEW MEXICO: The atomic bomb was tested.

26 July 1945
JAPAN: The Allies called for Japan's surrender: If not, the Japanese would face "prompt and utter destruction." Japan rejected the ultimatum.

6 August 1945
JAPAN: The U.S. dropped the atomic bomb on Hiroshima, unleashing death and destruction on a scale previously unimagined. At least 80,000 people died in the blast. Two days later, the bomb was dropped on Nagasaki, killing at least 35,000 people.

14 August 1945
UNITED STATES: President Harry Truman announced that Japan had accepted the Allies' terms of surrender.

2 September 1945
JAPAN: The formal surrender was signed. World War II was over.

DEATH TOLL

No one knows exactly how many people died in the Second World War. As in all wars, innocent men, women, and children were among the victims. But this war was like no other in the horrendous scale of suffering. Reasonable estimates put the death toll of both soldiers and civilians at somewhere between 45,000,000 and 50,000,000 human lives (including six million Jews who perished in the Holocaust).

▲ Cemeteries are vivid reminders of victory's cost. In a Canadian cemetery in Normandy, the gravestones of two brothers read:

"We left with a jest
Our homes in the west
Now here with the best
We lie at rest"

Axis	Military	Civilian	Total
Germany	3,500,000	700,000	4,200,000
Japan	2,000,000	350,000	2,350,000
Romania	300,000	160,000	460,000
Hungary	140,000	290,000	430,000
Italy	330,000	80,000	410,000
Austria	230,000	104,000	334,000
Finland	82,000	2,000	84,000
Axis total	**6,582,000**	**1,686,000**	**8,268,000**

Allies	Military	Civilian	Total
Russia	10,000,000	10,000,000	20,000,000
China	2,500,000	7,500,000	10,000,000
Poland	100,000	5,700,000	5,800,000
Yugoslavia	300,000	1,400,000	1,700,000
France	250,000	350,000	600,000
Czechoslovakia	200,000	215,000	415,000
United States	400,000	—	400,000
United Kingdom*	326,000	62,000	388,000
Netherlands	12,000	198,000	210,000
Greece	20,000	140,000	160,000
Belgium	12,000	76,000	88,000
Canada	37,000	—	37,000
India	24,000	13,000	37,000
Australia	23,000	12,000	35,000
Albania	28,000	2,000	30,000
Bulgaria	10,000	10,000	20,000
New Zealand	10,000	2,000	12,000
Norway	6,400	3,900	10,300
South Africa	7,000	—	7,000
Ethiopia	5,000	—	5,000
Luxembourg	5,000	—	5,000
Malta	—	2,000	2,000
Denmark	400	1,000	1,400
Brazil	1,000	—	1,000
Allies total	**14,276,800**	**25,686,900**	**39,963,700**
Est. war dead	**20,858,800**	**27,372,900**	**48,231,700**

* England, Scotland, Wales, and Northern Ireland

ACKNOWLEDGMENTS

Previously published accounts of John Spalding's section draw from one source: an interview with Spalding conducted on 9 February 1945. Valuable as this is document is, no one ever asked the other men for their version of events. By verifying their statements, and examining primary material, this story took shape. Many thanks are due . . .

To Sheila Heflin at the Kentucky Room (Daviess County Public Library) who gave me my first piece of information on John Spalding. To family members: Tina Spalding Gerteisen, Joe and Leonard Spalding, Stan Streczyk and Phyllis Streczyk Scheuermann, Mae Colwell, Steve Dzierga, Sophia Wozenski, and Eleanor Wozenski O'Rourke. To Glenn Hodges (Owensboro *Messenger-Inquirer*), Stanley E. Grabowski (Veterans Services, Harrison, New Jersey), James T. Parker III (Double Delta Industries), Andrew Woods (the 1st Division Museum), and to LTC Sion H. Harrington III (North Carolina Division of Archives and History). To the staff and facilities of the Urban Archives (Temple University), the Military History Institute (Carlisle Barracks), the Commonwealth War Graves Commission (Canadian Agency), the Beaver County Research Center (Carnegie Library), the Passaic Public Library, the Chattanooga-Hamilton County Bicentennial Library, the D-Day Museum, the New York Public Library, and the National Archives. To LTC Steven L. Clay and Col. Rene C. Provost. To friends, researchers, and colleagues Lynn Weingarten, Roy Reiss, Sarah Wuerth, Chuck Solomon, Scott MacNeill, Irene Lipton, Grey Thornberry, Kathy Kiernan, James Du, and Peter John. To Brooke Goffstein for her insight and support. And, above all, to Clarence Colson, Fred Reese, Stan Dzierga, Walt Bieder, Bruce Buck, and Vinny DiGaetano.

Books

American Forces in Action Series: Omaha Beachhead, 6 June-13 June 1944 (Washington, D.C., War Department Historical Division, 1945)

Martin Blumenson, *United States Army in World War II: The European Theater of Operations: Breakout and Pursuit* (Washington, D.C., Government Printing Office, 1961)

Hugh M. Cole, *United States Army in World War II: The European Theater of Operations: The Ardennes: Battle of the Bulge* (Washington, D.C., Government Printing Office, 1963)

I.C.B. Dear, *The Oxford Companion to World War Two* (Oxford University Press, 1995)

Gregory Frumkin, *Population Changes in Europe Since 1939* (New York, Augustus M. Kelley, Inc., 1951)

Kent Roberts Greenfield, et. al., *United States Army in World War II: The Army Ground Forces: The Organization of Ground Combat Troops* (Washington, D.C., Historical Division Dept. of the Army, 1947)

Gordon A. Harrison, *United States Army in World War II: The European Theater of Operations: Cross Channel Attack* (Washington, D.C., Government Printing Office, 1951)

Charles B. MacDonald, *United States Army in World War II: The European Theater of Operations: The Siegfried Line Campaign* (Washington, D.C., Government Printing Office, 1963)

Samuel Eliot Morison, *History of United States Naval Operations in World War II, Vol. I: The Battle of the Atlantic, September 1939-May 1943; Vol. XI: The Invasion of France and Germany, 1944-1945* (Boston, Little, Brown and Company, 1975)

J. David Singer and Melvin Small, *The Wages of War 1816-1965: A Statistical Handbook* (New York, John Wiley and Sons Inc., 1972)

Samuel A. Stouffer, et. al., *Studies in Social Psychology in World War Two: The American Soldier: Adjustment During Army Life, Vol. I; Combat and Its Aftermath, Vol. II* (Princeton University Press, 1949)

B. Urlanis, *Wars and Population* (Moscow, Progress Publishers, 1971)

Mary H. Williams, *United States Army in World War II: Special Studies: Chronology 1941-1945* (Washington, D.C., Government Printing Office, 1960)

Official records

Reports were submitted by units throughout the war. They are immensely valuable to researchers, and are housed in the National Archives. The 16th Regiment reports can be found in Record Group 407.

Combat interviews and narratives

The army's Historical Division interviewed soldiers after combat. The 16-page transcript that resulted from John Spalding's interview is a basic source for anyone writing about D-Day. My copy came from the collection at the Military History Institute (Carlisle Barracks, Pennsylvania). I am also grateful to the Imperial War Museum, Sound Archives (London, England) for a recorded interview conducted with Ed Wozenski (accession number 3014/2/1).

Unpublished materials and interviews

Families have preserved documents that were invaluable. Tina Spalding Gerteisen was especially generous with copies of John's letters, his service records, and medical report. Sophia Wozenski, Eleanor Wozenski O'Rourke, Mae Colwell, and Phyllis Streczyk Scheuermann shared materials and reminisces. I also spent many hours with Clarence Colson, Fred Reese, Stan Dzierga, Walt Bieder, Bruce Buck, and Vinny DiGaetano. I especially appreciate their cooperation in recalling the painful past (other men of Spalding's section were contacted and refused).

If you have information about any of the soldiers mentioned in this book, please contact the author at WarChronicle.com.